Oh Lord, Tell Me Why

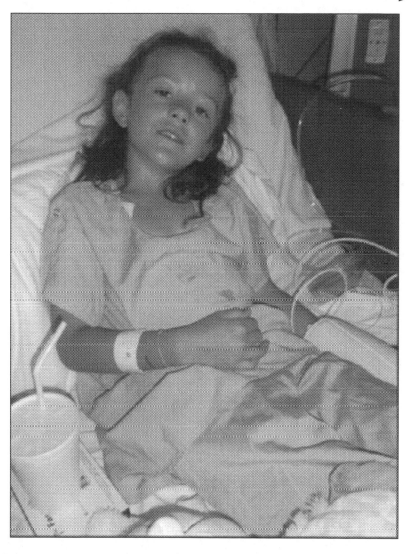

Poetic Inspirational Stories
Written By Gary L Tucker

ISBN: 978-1-4669-0322-7 (sc)
ISBN: 978-1-4669-0321-0 (e)

Trafford rev. 11/09/2011

 www.trafford.com

North America & international
toll-free: 1 888 232 4444 (USA & Canada)
phone: 250 383 6864 ♦ fax: 812 355 4082

Contents

Oh Lord, Tell Me Why

About the book

This book is filled with contemporary poems written as mini short stories with a message. A few are waiting for someone to attach a melody, perhaps you. Here you will find poems that help draw you close to God. A few poems were written to honor the many who have fought and sacrificed with their lives for this great country, The United States of America.

I wish to extend special thanks to Ronald Pearce for his service to this great country as he and his four brothers traveled the world as soldiers in the United States Army. To the Pearce brothers and all who choose a life of servitude I offer a heart felt thank you.

You can read an expanded version of my poems in **I'm Feelin' Kinda Gassy**, which includes all of these poems plus fun poems, romantic poems with a twist and some about life's lessons.

Thank you, Gary Tucker

Edited and photo arrangements by Gary Tucker.

Inspirational
Poems

Oh Lord, Tell Me Why

Little girl don't you cry
Little boy dry your eyes
I know you're asking why
Oh Lord, tell me why.

The pain you try to hide
Reveals the hurt inside
When heartaches come in tides
You loose all sense of pride.

Don't be afraid if you can't walk
You need fingers to help you talk
When others point and gawk
Rise above them and don't sulk.

The disease that lives inside
An awful sickness there abides
Its growth does not subside
With medications you have tried.

If your eyes don't let you see
You get lost along your way
When the sun cannot be seen
I'll guide you to a brighter day.

When your mind is working slow
And it's hard for you to think
Take my hand and I will show
You how to bridge the link.

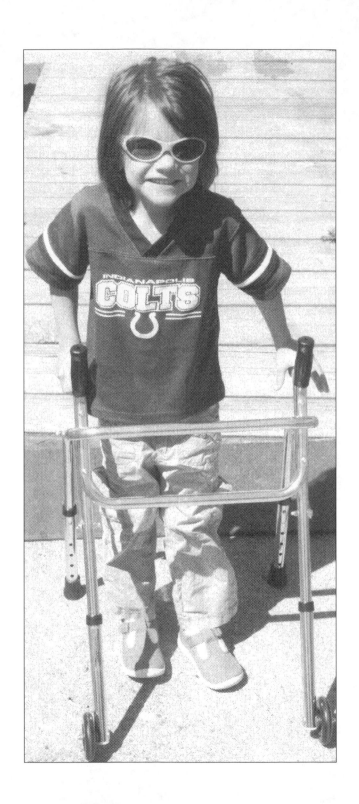

Little girl don't you cry
Little boy dry your eyes
I know you're asking why
Oh Lord, tell me why.

The imperfections we all share
Will some day fade away
New bodies with new clothes we'll wear
Come resurrection day.

No more loneliness or sorrow
Or cloudy days of rain
Look forward to tomorrow
We have so much to gain.

We'll no longer live in pain
No longer feel ashamed
We'll be smarter than any mortal
With new ingenious brains.

We'll play hide and seek
And throw a super fastball
Never tire; never sleep
Skip rope and that's not all.

We'll run and jump to the sky
We'll even learn how to fly
Our new bodies never die
We'll stop asking why.

We'll have new tongues for voicing
No need to speak with hands
With new ears will hear rejoicing
Throughout all the land.

If you wish to find relief
From your suffering and grief
A glorious day awaits you
If in Jesus you believe.

Special ones with special needs
Deserve a special love
When a hand is reaching out in need
Remember, God's watching from above. ⊠

Written by Gary Tucker
3-4-2011
©

As I was walking along in the mall a hand reached out to me. Looking at the face of this man I could tell he had special needs. I was honored to shake his hand. This ode is in honor of him. For those who believe, there really is some truth in the story of Superman.

Second Chances

He failed over and over again
No one gave him second chances
Before judging others
Consider your own circumstances.

If you think you're perfect
You're not alone
There's a long line of critics
Waiting to cast the first stone.

It's hard to say, "I'm sorry"
It's harder to say, "I forgive you"
You've been given second chances
Forgive the past and start anew.

When I was passed out in gutters
God gave me second chances
He left His ninety-nine to find me
Where no one dared to glance.

I was not in full agreement
When I prayed to be delivered
Because of insincerity
My prayers were unheard.

Another day out of my head
I wasted so many years
The pain I felt from the loneliness
Caused so many tears.

I created a place
Which no one could enter
I didn't have to grow up
A fantasy world was rendered.

Back in nineteen eighty-four
God again knocked on my door
Sincerely I said, "Please, help me Lord,"
Now I have so much to be thankful for.

An addiction is beyond understanding
To the wise who have not entered in
Behind stonewalls they say
"Thank God I'm not like him."

They worship their exotic spirits
While abusing medical pills
Sitting on their judgment thrones
Unaware of their own ills.

Only a heart of love can truly see
Another's pain and agony
Free from your suffering you may be
If you truly want recovery.

I failed over and over again
But, I was given second chances
Before judging others
I consider my own circumstances. ©

Written by Gary Tucker 1-6-2011 ©

Acknowledgement, Desire, Recovery Matt. 7:1-5, Luke 15:4-7,
Luke 15:11-32

Journey Home Inspired by my aunt Beverly

Started out I wasn't feeling so well
Then the doctor had some news to tell
"You don't have much time, I'm so sorry"
I said to my friend "Let's have a party."

I want to see all my family, all my friends
Before my time here comes to an end
It may sound crude, but I've been blessed
From this frail body I'll have sweet rest.

Each painful day I'm drawn closer to my Lord
Some day this body will be restored
As my body grows weaker God's love seems stronger
I keep asking how much longer.

I'm looking forward to my journey home
It's good to know I won't travel alone
An angel from heaven will come for me
To take me where my Lord I'll see.

My new home is beyond the sky
I'll be there before you blink an eye
Gates of pearls and streets of gold
In my new home no one grows old.

I like to think I'll see you there
But, what Jesus said is very clear
"Unless you love Me and I dwell in your heart
"The glories of heaven you'll have no part."

There's no guarantee when it comes to living
Real life only comes when God is forgiving
Ask Jesus to save you and do it fast
This day, today may be your last.

Hope to see you on the other side
Where peace, love and joy abide
The choice is yours and yours alone
Follow me to a heavenly home.

I'm looking forward to my journey home
It's good to know I won't travel alone
With many others who've been atoned
Going to heaven where I'll never roam.

My heavenly home is beyond the sky
I'll be there before you blink an eye
Praising Jesus in all His glory
Forever thankful for the gospel story.

I'm looking forward to my journey home
It's good to know I won't travel alone
My heavenly home is beyond the sky
I'll be there before you blink an eye. ©

Written by Gary Tucker
9-2-2010
©

You'll Find Me
When You're Looking Down

When will you trust me, you know that I care
You're to blind to see your life's in despair
You want to live free but life isn't fair
I know your needs, more anguish you'll bear.

I love you more than all the sparrows
Walk in my path, its straight and narrow
Stay the course and there'll be no more sorrow
Not many more breaths you may borrow.

When life's too much for you to bear
Humble yourself and I'll be there
Abundant grace with you I'll share
Then you'll see how much I care.

When you think I'm nowhere to be found
You'll find me when you face the ground
Come to me where life abounds
You'll find me when you're looking down.

You say you're broke, I see what you're buying
To you life's a joke, soon you'll be crying
There's manna before you but you won't bend down
How much did you loose when you went up town?

It may be dull and yes it is dingy
Your heart says, "I need more than a penny"
You walk by it with a proud glance
I sent you some money; you took your stance.

When life's too much for you to bear
Humble yourself and I'll be there
Abundant grace with you I'll share
Then you'll see how much I care.

When you think I'm nowhere to be found
You'll find me when you face the ground
Come to me where life abounds
You'll find me when you're looking down.

I gave my life so you can live
A love for me you won't give
I feed you, cloth you, cover your head
When will you realize your soul is dead?

You love your life more than me
From your sins you must flee
Open you heart and you will see
Eternal life comes only from me.

When life's too much for you to bear
Humble yourself and I'll be there
Abundant grace with you I'll share.
Then you'll see how much I care.

When you think I'm nowhere to be found
You'll find me when you face the ground
Come to me where life abounds
You'll find me when you're looking down.

Humble yourself and I'll be there
You'll find me when you face the ground
Then you'll see how much I care
You'll find me when you're looking down. ©
Written by Gary Tucker © 9-2-2010

Army, Navy, Air Force, Marines

Written by Gary Tucker © 8-6-2011

I'm proud to serve like my father before me
And fight with others to defend our country
No matter the challenge or trying condition
Beside my brothers it's a family tradition.

I may speak soft but carry big stick
When under attack I respond quick
To my enemy I say be forewarned
Marching to battle in my army uniform.

Sailing swiftly upon the high seas
More relentless than a nest of honey bees
When alarm bells ring feel her mighty sting
There's no escape from vengeance she flings.

Caves don't protect and if you ask why
No one hides from eagles in the sky
From many miles and x-ray vision eyes
When she drops her eggs be prepared to die.

The enemy can't hide under cover of night
Agile Marines have them in their sights
When they think they're safe and secure
Fierce judgment is speedily procured.

We know some won't return with the rest
They sacrificed their lives giving their best
Never forgotten though they be gone
With heart felt gratitude their memories live on.

As long as I have breath and strength to stand
I'll defend my country with gun in hand
With God as my friend I'll continue the fight
Defeating the enemy with holy might.

Weather Army, Navy, Air Force, Marines
No one stands against this fighting machine
Keeping the peace and protecting the week
I'm honored to defend what the oppressed seek. ©

UNITED STATES ARMY

Benjamin

Jack

Robert

Russell

Ronald

Meet
the
Pearce
Brothers

American Heroes

Gary Tucker

Hills of Tennessee

I'm going home to the hills of Tennessee
I miss regal mountains where eagles soar free
When I can't walk and my eyes can't see
Carry me home to the hills of Tennessee.

There I'll lie still next to Father and Mother
Slumber in peace with Sister and Brother
I long to rest in the shadow of her hills
From valleys to peeks they are glory filled.

Her noble tips are crowned in royal smoke
As creeks flow gracefully down forest slopes
There's a place in my heart for Tennessee hills
When my final breath fades I'll love her still.

I'm going home to the hills of Tennessee
I miss regal mountains where eagles soar free
When I can't walk and my eyes can't see
Carry me home to the hills of Tennessee.

I'll take my last ride up that crooked dirt road
Over clear running streams to my new abode
The mountains await me for a long embrace
Until our creator returns with sweet grace.

Toward the east I'll see the morning star rise
Lighting the way for my Lord in the sky
Weep not for me 'cause I know what's in store
When my Master calls I'll rise alive evermore.

I'm going home to the hills of Tennessee
I miss regal mountains where eagles soar free
When I can't walk and my eyes can't see
Carry me home to the hills of Tennessee.

When I can't walk and my eyes can't see
Burry my bones in the hills of Tennessee. ©

Written by Gary Tucker
2-16-2011 ©

John the Baptist

Written by Gary Tucker 2-7-2011 ©
Luke 1, Matt 11: 1-19, Matt 14: 1-12

The birth of a prophet was foretold with explicit clues
Now is the time for this prophesy to come true
Within wombs of two women are Jesus and John
Two cousins born Spirit filled as time pressed on.

Elizabeth and Zacharias were old and with out child
They prayed to God and in time upon them He smiled
God opened her womb and there a son was conceived
With much love and joy baby John was received.

When he became of age he preached under the dessert sun
Baptizing believers and preparing the way for The Holy One
He wore a camel skin for clothing feeding on locust and honey
He had no house, mule, or land, not one coin for money.

He preached repentance of sins without flattery words
This angered Queen Herodias because of the truth she heard
She was unlawfully married to her king and begged to have him killed
The king refused but had him jailed until another prophesy fulfilled.

Herodias had a lovely daughter trained in seductive dance
Herod offered half his kingdom if he and his guest could have a glance
Mother and daughter conspired agreeing this was their chance
So she danced for the king until he yielded in hypnotic trance.

As agreed demanding of the king, "Upon your oath I now insist,
Deliver to me on a platter the head of John the Baptist."
The evil king was grieved, but granted her despicable request
He certainly couldn't renege on a promise witnessed by his guest.

That same night the ax fell and John's blood was spilled
The wicked queen eagerly waited to see the kings' order filled
She finally got what she longed for without even a fuss
John the Baptist is the greatest prophet there ever was. ©

I Believe I've Just Been Born Again

The preaching was strong
Powerful words not heard in so long
His message was contrary to the life I'd built
My soul felt heavy from the weight of guilt.

The sermon was over and he began to pray
"Heavenly Father, thank you for this glorious day
"Thank you for saving us in such a marvelous way
"Maybe there's someone here who's soul you'll save."

As I looked up I could see
The preacher was staring right at me
He said, "Let go of your sin
"And today you can be born again."

But, I held tight to the pew before me
I was afraid of what might be
"Do not delay and you can be free"
All the while he's looking at me.

The organ pipes were ringing
To the congregation's heart felt singing
"Just one more verse", I heard
"Then we'll have a closing word."

The organ pipes stopped ringing
As the congregation stopped singing
Then someone yelled out to say
"Wait for me I want to be saved today."

As I made my way up the isle
I was greeted by his smile
Said, "We've been praying for you Mr. Penn
"Are you ready to be born again?"

The organ pipes started ringing
To the congregation's heart felt singing
There were loud Hallelujahs and shouts of Amen
I believe, I believe, I've just been born again.

I believe, I believe, I've just been born again. ©

Written by Gary Tucker
10-30-2010
©

Old Time Religion

Written by Gary Tucker 12-14-2010 ©

I'm going to an old time convention
To get some of that old time religion
The kind preached without detention
With intensions of a heavenly ascension.

Sitting in church pews week after week
Believing what every smooth talker speaks
Without opening the Bible to take a peek
They're deceived by wolves dressed as sheep.

Sitting in church pews month after month
The gospel of Christ preached not once
Holding souls ransom as she teaches subtle lies
Unaware of deception she's a devil in disguise.

Sitting in church pews year after year
Life saving Word withheld from their ears
Forsaking the truth they once held dear
Their eternal destiny is evidently clear.

So many churches have doused their light
There's no truth left in them to shine bright
To blind to see the condition of their plight
Their robes are spotted and no longer white.

So many churches across this land
With many names and different brands
They've become bacons of great wealth
At our expense through cleverness and stealth.

Why are churches lifeless and unspiritual?
It's because dead souls desire only a ritual
I'm going back to that old time religion
Because there's no hope in this new age rendition.

I'm going to an old time convention
To get some of that old time religion
The kind preached without detention
With intensions of a heavenly ascension. ©

Wish

Wish I had a voice to sing of God's abundant glory
I'd sing of His majesty and His redeeming story.

Wish I could write songs about God's graces
I'd write pages and pages to last through the ages.

Wish I could preach the gospel without reservation
I'd let the truth I speak convince people with persuasion.

Wish I had enough faith to walk upon water
I'd one step at a time walk closer to the Father.

Wish I had patience like Job when facing trials
I'd be more willing for my neighbor to walk an extra mile.

Wish I had a heart of love and compassion to offer
I'd reach out to others with help and words softer.

Wish I had courage like David facing the giant
I'd go out into the world showing the gospel to be reliant.

Wish I had strength like Samson fending off so many men
I'd be willing to fight righteous battles over and over again.

Wish I had wisdom like Salomon discerning right from wrong
I'd be able to make right decisions without taking so long.

Wish all these attributes I now attain
I'd be less inclined to whine and complain. ©

Written by Gary Tucker
11-21-2010 ©

What More Do I Need?

I have pillows on my bed
A roof over my head
I have a job that pays the bills
Suffer from no ills.

I'm so rich in this life
With friends and good wife
I have God's Word that feeds me
Why should I feel needy?

I don't need a fancy car
Or an airplane to fly me far
I don't need a lovely mansion
For worldly things I have no passion.

I don't need expensive clothes
At clearance sales I buy the most
I don't need a hefty bankroll
My soul might pay a heavy toll.

I don't worry about things to earthly
In a heavenly kingdom I'll live eternally
I don't lose sleep trying to count sheep
In blissful peace I always sleep.

I have angels watching over me
Some day their faces I'll see
I have God's love indeed
What more do I need? ©

Written by Gary Tucker
11-21-2010 ©

A Man From Galilee

(An Easter drama)

Choir
God loved us so much He sent His Holy Son
Whoever believes in Him will see a miracle done
His Spirit will renew us as lifeless souls become alive
Eternal death will loose its grip and Holiness will thrive.

The Immortal Son left Heaven to bare the sins of man
Retaining deity as man fulfilling Salvation's plan
Many words were written as the future was foretold
He walked among us thirty-three years as prophecies unfolded.

The Blessed Son has many names; perhaps you've heard of one
He is the great I AM, Savior, Christ and Holy One
He is Emanuel, Prince of Peace, a Mighty God to fear
Messiah, Counselor, King and others you'll soon hear.

Listen to this story for every word is true
He made a way to Heaven especially for you
Clear your mind and open your heart
Let today be the day you make a new start.

Narrator
There came a man from Galilee
Said He came to set men free
Born of a virgin without aid of earthly father
He came into this world to die upon an alter.

In Him is Life and a Light shining for all men
Because of darkness in men they could not comprehend
He is Alpha and Omega, the beginning and end
Broken relations with men He set out to mend.

Speaking in parables God's Word to proclaim
In Him men have hope; Jesus is His name
The poor became rich hearing Him preach
With wisdom and power He did teach.

He taught us how to live and go about our day
The purpose of life and how to God we should pray
We need not worry about things so earthly
He taught us what it meant to be spiritually worthy.

The lame He made walk and the blind to see
Others were possessed but Jesus set them free
The dead He made alive and limbs to grow
Bodies were deformed now look at them glow.

Diseases He healed and changed water into wine
Ears were unhearing but now they hear fine
He had a heart of love and spoke with God's authority
The people who loved Him were sadly the minority.

Performing miracles all the people to Him ran
But, the jealous Pharisees made an evil plan
They arrested Him and took Him by hand
Death to this Holy man was their demand.

Caiaphas asked Jesus, "Is it true what I heard?"
Before the high priest He said not a word
"I adjure You, Are You the Christ, the Son of God?"
"You have said it yourself," Jesus replied with a nod.

The high priest was so furious he tore his robe
They found their excuse; no need to further probe
"He's guilty of blasphemy; now He must die!"
This was their plan; they believed their own lie.

They took Him to Pilate, a governor of Rome
The deeds of a criminal he mustn't condone
They presented their lies and demanded he condemn
Pilate saw through them and found no fault in Him.

The governor spoke to have Jesus freed
But, the Pharisees wouldn't overcome their greed
Pilate offered the mob a trade in lieu
Barabbas, a killer or Jesus, King Of The Jews.

A fair offer the Jews did not perceive
How could they when they did not believe
The mob chose a killer to be set free
Pilate sent Jesus to die on a tree.

With a battered body and a crown of thorns
Marching to Golgotha to endure more scorn
It is written, "On behalf of the people one man must die"
Upon this lonely hill God's Lamb would be crucified.

Along with Jesus two other men hung
One mocking and one confessing with tongue
"Jesus, when You come into Your Kingdom, remember me"
Jesus replied, "With Me in Paradise Today you'll be."

Suffering on the cross this battle will soon be won
There's no other way for the Father's will to be done?
In agony He prayed to the Father that we be forgiven
While guards gambled for His garments to see what they'd be given.

Many gathered to watch the Lamb of God die
This was the Master's plan but no one understood why
The religious hypocrites were there mocking in fun
Saying, "Save Yourself if You truly are the Chosen One."

Then a cloud of darkness overtook the day
For the sins of the world a horrific price God will pay
"My God, My God, Why Have You Forsaken Me?"
"It Is Finished." With His final breath Jesus died to set men free.

As the demons were prowling the wind began howling
A loud crack spit the sky as angels could only stand by
How can man be justified by this One being crucified?
All heaven's host watched as He gave up the Ghost.

The earth was veiled in darkness to hide such pain and misery
Separation of Father from Son caused much anxiety
Jesus remained sinless to the very end
But the Father couldn't look upon Him because on Him lay my sin.

When Jesus said, "It is finished", Satan thought he'd won
He assumed the battle was finally over with the Blessed One
With temporary satisfaction he danced 'round Deaths' hill
Only an unholy mind could find such death a thrill.

Then the earth shook and rocks were split.
From top to bottom the temple veil ripped
On Him God's wrath was poured without filter
The human cost was only thirty pieces of silver.

It was getting late so the Pharisees rushed things along
Complaining to Pilate, The criminals' deaths is taking to long
It's against our law for them to hang past three
Send guards to break legs of those hanging on trees.

Pilate sent word to guards on the hill
Proceed breaking legs at your discretion and will
They came to Jesus and found Him already dead
A guard pierced Him with a spear instead.

As was prophesized He had not a broken bone
From the cross to the tomb to be buried alone
The Pharisees asked Pilate to guard the tomb three days
So His disciples couldn't steal His body away.

After the Sabbath toward the fist day of the week
Came ladies named Mary; a look at the grave they seek
A severe earthquake occurred and an angle appeared
The guards became as dead and shook with great fear.

His appearance was like lightning with clothes white as snow
"What's happening here?" The women wanted to know
The angel rolled away the tombstone and then sat down
"He has risen, don't be afraid" to look around.

There were other tombs opened and saints were raised
Walking down city streets giving God all the praise
Now you would suppose this event would be much heard
So much happened in only thirty-four short words.

"Go tell His disciples He has risen from the dead
"He'll meet them in Galilee", not far up ahead
The sting of death men no longer need to fear
When they see Jesus It will all be made clear.

When Jesus met His disciples He explained His Father's will
"All things written of Me by the prophets must be fulfilled
"How I would suffer and rise from the dead the third day"
To die on a cross for mankind was the price I willingly paid.

He led them to Bethany after speaking these words
And blessing them He ascended from this world
With great joy the disciples worshipped Him
And continually praised God in song and hymns.

Disciple's song
He's alive, He has risen
Man can now be forgiven
He arose from the grave
Mankind can now be saved.

Glory to God, a new day has dawned
Praise to Jesus new life can spawn
When earthly bodies have expired
Judgment on the saved is not required.

The serpent thought he prevailed
When Jesus to the cross was nailed
What the devil didn't realize
From the grave He soon would rise.

As hard as demons tried
They could not prevent His rise
He's no longer on Death's side
Jesus Christ is glorified.

The Prince of Peace arose
He arose, He arose
The tomb could not contain Him
Shout it out, He arose.

Praise the Father, Praise the Son
Praise the Spirit, three in one
Praise the Father, Praise the Son
Praise the Spirit, Holy One.

Narrator
Twenty centuries have since passed and the story hasn't changed
The way to the Father through Jesus remains the same
If you repent from your sins and believe in His Holy name
You may dwell in Heaven without guilt or shame.

Our bodies are frail and grow so tired
We don't have much time before they expire
What we do in this life will decide our eternal fate
Ask Jesus to save you now before it's too late. ©

Written by Gary Tucker
2-7-2011
©

My Prayer

Written By Gary Tucker © 10-10-2010

Lord, please forgive me and hear my prayer
My broken heart is in need of repair
Extend your mercy and correct me from err
The guilt of my transgression is too much to bear.

You are the Almighty and one true God
You made all there is with less than a nod
You rule all creation with an outstretched rod
You watch over your children wherever they trod.

I've been the target of fierce fiery darts
Tempting me they've pierced my heart
From righteous ways I chose to part
To confess more sins, where shall I start?

The lust of my flesh I'm unable to tame
Day after day I sink deeper in shame
Disregarding Your Holy name
Parting myself from Your splendor and fame.

Lord, please forgive me and hear my prayer
My broken heart is in need of repair
Extend your mercy and correct me from err
The guilt of my transgression is too much to bear.

I use to walk close to you in Holy ways
Now I go my way and further I stray
I use to love You and do as You say
I use to look forward to a glorious day.

I want to do right, but I'm weak with no might
I long for peace, but its nowhere in sight
I've lost my way, alone in the night
Lord, I surrender I give up the fight.

Please restore me to the apple of Your eye
Guide me back home as you listen to me cry
Keep me safe in Your hand where Satan can't pry
Without your protection most surely I'd die.

Lord, please forgive me and hear my prayer
My broken heart is in need of repair
Extend your mercy and correct me from err
The guilt of my transgression is too much to bear.

Lord, you are omniscient, nothing's unknown
You are omnipotent, Strong Cornerstone
There's no hidden place unseen from Your throne
Thank you Lord, all my sins You atoned. ©

When The Trumpet Sounds

When the trumpet sounds
Calling saints from the ground
Forsaking Death's shroud
To ascend through the clouds.

Far above earthly heights
To Heaven gleaming bright
Brighter than the stars
Its brilliance has no par.

Men's words can't describe
The grandeur viewed inside
Out of mortal's reach
Made with golden streets.

Standing face to face
With The King of Grace
Crowned with diadems
All knees bow to Him

From His Holy Throne
Jesus calls His own
Giving us new names
No two are the same.

All tongues shall confess
All creatures shall profess
Resounding evermore
Jesus Christ is Lord.

When the trumpet sounds
Calling saints from the ground
Forsaking Death's shroud
To ascend through the clouds.

In harmonic voice
Saints sing and rejoice
Adoration loudly raise
As angels lend their praise.

Upon Golgotha's hill
Prophesies were fulfilled
Jesus was nailed to a cross
To redeem mankind lost.

He suffered there until
His death paid Ransom's bill
Taking my place to die
So I'd be made alive.

He redeems men that find
Release from sin that binds
With salvation freely given
Forgiving them their sins.

When cursed was my soul
God's love overflowed
Transforming a sinful heart
With holiness He imparts.

From two choices one make
When your soul is at stake
God offers life eternal
Sin offers death's infernal.

Won't you choose life?
And become a Holy wife
Partake of this mystery
As God's bride for eternity.

When the trumpet sounds
Calling saints from the ground
Forsaking Death's shroud
To ascend through the clouds.

In harmonic voice
Saints sing and rejoice
Adoration loudly raise
As angels lend their praise.

Jesus Christ is Lord
We adore Him evermore
To God be the glory
For what He did for me. ©

Written by Gary Tucker
7-15-2011
©

Starry Night

Starry night
Shining bright
Shedding light
Glorious sight.

Words of old
Had foretold
In the land
Of Bethlehem.

God's own son
The Chosen One
Came to men
His work defend.

Followed the star
From distance far
Came royal kings
Gifts to bring.

With much delight
Embraced the Light
Filled with joy
Seeing the Boy.

As then still now
The wise still bow
Presenting gifts
In morning mist.

Starry night
Shining bright
Shedding light
Glorious sight.

Starry night
Shining bright
Lighting the way
Men to save.

Words of old
Had foretold
Don't you know?
Blood must flow.

God's own son
Almighty One
On altar's cross
Suffered the cost.

Follow the star
From distance far
Escape prison bars
Where you are.

With much delight
Embrace the Light
Compelled to be
On bended knees.

As then still now
The wise still bow
Goodness persist
Gainst evil resist.

Starry night
Shining bright
Shedding light
Glorious sight.

Starry night
Shining bright
In our hearts
May it start.

Words of old
Had foretold
Breaking chains
Souls reclaimed.

God's own son
The Holy One
From sins be
Setting me free.

Followed the star
From distance far
Old life concedes
New life conceived.

With much delight
Embraced the light
I can rejoice
Triumphant voice.

As then still now
The wise still bow
Prayers I lift
As Spirit sifts.

Starry night
Shining bright
Shedding light
Glorious sight. ©
Written by Gary Tucker 8-2-2011 ©

New Jerusalem

Revelations 21, 22

With Heaven's gates open wide
Inviting saints to come inside
Hues of color not viewed by mortals
As we enter through pearly portals.

We'll walk on golden streets like glass
After walls of precious stones we pass
Made of jasper, sapphires and emeralds
New Jerusalem will radiate eternal.

As we're surrounded by Holy Light
Majestic creatures direct in flight
Pointing the way for all who enter
Guiding us toward smoke at the center.

As I come close I see a wondrous sight
From a throne shoots rays of light
A beautiful rainbow circles all 'round
As peals of thunder continually sound.

Upon the throne sits the Son of Man
With bronze feet should He choose to stand
His head and hair are white like snow
From His face comes the brightest glow.

I hear supreme power in His voice
Like the sound of many waters making noise
Anything tainted with sin or defies
Would be consumed by His fiery eyes.

Before Him I fall down as a lifeless man
In His presence I'm to scared to stand
Then to experience something so grand
Upon me God places His right hand.

"I'm the One who died and forever is alive
I'm Alfa and Omega, here you shall reside"
"Do not be afraid," I will hear Him say,
"I Am that I Am welcomes you here today".

Within His reach is the book of life
Containing names redeemed by the Light
All the saints will be given new names
And immortal bodies free of sin's chains.

From His throne flows water of life
Next to the river is the tree of life
Bearing twelve kinds of fruit to eat
Its healing leaves will nations reap.

There will no longer be any curse
Creation will be free of sinful lures
His words are faithful and they are true
God will again make all things new.

This is the day when saints rejoice
In unison sing with praiseful voice
Eternal life and happiness received
Reserved for those who in Jesus believed. ©

Written by Gary Tucker
9-15-2011

Be Strong in The Lord

Ephesians 6
Written by Gary Tucker 9-30-2011 ©

Prepare your feet to take a battle stand
With the gospel of peace firm in hand
Proclaim the Word throughout the land
For this is our Lord's command.

The gospel is a mysterious waste
To multitudes with lifeless souls
Pray for boldness to move with haste
So new life all mankind may know.

Be strong and courageous in the Lord
Advancing in His all powerful might
Be suited with God's protective armor
Prepare yourselves for a spiritual fight.

We struggle not with flesh and blood
But against rulers of a spiritual realm
Upon all creation their evil floods
With the great deceiver at their helm.

When the prince of darkness aims at you
Lift high your shield of faith
Stand firm girded in light and truth
Knowing only God's word can save.

Put on the helmet of salvation
To deflect deadly blows to your head
Use the Spirit's sword in anticipation
Against them that desire such dread.

Pray in the Spirit with un-blurred intuition
Laying before the alter humble supplications
Remain alert with perseverance and resolution
Working toward the day of our restoration.

Pray for ambassadors in willing chains
Preaching in confidence with His protection
Pray the Spirit guide you so you may attain
Life eternal magnifying His glorious perfection.

From our Creator the Father of love
And His blessed Son Jesus Christ
Peace be to saintly sisters and brothers
Grace rest upon you from Him on High. ©

Oh, Mighty God A Sinner's Prayer

Oh, Mighty God I cry out to Thee
With a contrite heart hear my plea
Covered in shame and sinful stains
Naked and dirty bound by chains.

I come before You as a vessel of clay
Mold me and shape in Your perfect way
Only You know the sum of my days
Before barrowed time in this life fades.

I'm so thirsty and my soul is dry
Only drink from Your Fountain will satisfy
My body trembles with hunger panes
Only Your Bread of Life can sustain.

Forgive sinful deeds of my days past
Help me now perform works that last
Upon the alter I place selfish desires
As burdens are lifted like smoke from fire.

Look upon me now with merciful eyes
See a repentant man reaching toward the sky
Speak the words my ears long to hear
Say You forgive me in a way so clear.

Oh, Mighty God great are Your works
So many examples besides this earth
I ask You to perform a greater work in me
Make me Your servant counted as worthy.

I worship You and glorify Your name
From this day on I shall never be the same
You alone set me free with loving mercy
Renewing my life in preparation for eternity. ©
Written by Gary Tucker © 10-1-2011

Friend,

Does Oh, Mighty God have any meaning for you? We are all born sinners bound by deathly chains. Some have been freed and received eternal life. Have you been released from chains that keep you separated from God? Only Merciful God can set us free. Does your soul feel dried up and lifeless? Do you hunger for something but find nothing fills you? Do you think you've committed so many sins that you can't be forgiven? The number of past sins makes no difference. Right now where you are make this your prayer in all sincerity. Ask God to forgive you for all sins past because only holy deeds will last. If this is your first sincere prayer then this is your first holy deed. May you now begin to glorify God with many good works, praises and thanksgivings as He prepares you for your journey to eternity.

Valley of Fear

When you're in the valley of fear
And the road to peace is unclear
Life gives you more than you can bear
Call on a friend who is so dear.

When God's love seems so far away
No hope of getting through the day
Be still and listen to what I say
Bow your head and begin to pray.

When nothing seems to be going right
At the end of the tunnel you see no light
All you want is some rest tonight
Then pray to God with all your might.

When your life seems so pitiful poor
There's never enough and you need more
Pick yourself up off the floor
Just ask Jesus to open His store.

When you're in a fiery lake
And eternal life is at stake
The best decision you can make
Trust in Jesus your soul to take.

When you feel you're all alone
Among friends or even at home
When you're feeling tempted to roam
Trust in Jesus, the Cornerstone.

When you feel completely lost
From wave to wave you're being tossed
You want peace at any cost
Call on Jesus; He saves the lost.

When you feel you're on the hook
For something you haven't forsook
Read all about it in the Good Book
Turn the pages; it's worth a look.

When you feel life is unreal
What you do is no big deal
What you need is a spiritual meal
Feed on the Word; your soul it will heal.

When you feel you're under the gun
There's no place for you to run
In the shadows away from the sun
Turn to the Light, the Holy One. ©

Written by Gary Tucker
9-2-2010
©

I Pledge My Allegiance

Written by Gary Tucker 3-16-2011 ©

I stand at attention sincerely glad
As I pledge my allegiance to this flag
Symbolizing a republic for which she stands
Casting rays of independence over her land.

A fruited and bountiful land indivisible
Granting inalienable rights to individuals
Upon sovereign staff she waves free each day
Many mortals died to keep her this way.

A mighty nation under the guidance of God
His mercy protects her with a corrective rod
Constantly striving divine goals to reach
For instruction and virtues humbly beseech.

Outside her borders are heard amazing stories
Falling on captive ears yearning for her glories
Answering freedom's call to her they flee
Risking their lives crossing turbulent seas.

Declarations of liberty and justice resound
Free from oppression many have found
Finding equality and security within her stars
And peace received under red and white bars.

When Old Glory flies free and unfurled
Her colors reflect hope to an entire world
When asked what these colors acclaim
The United States of America proclaim.

When laws are righteous and judgment fair
Subjects live free and not in despair
When laws are corrupt and too heavy to bear
Peace and tranquility are viewed nowhere.

On bended knee I pray God's love for her endures
I will honor those who died keeping her pure
Upon my shoulders her burdens I'll gladly bear
May Stars and Stripes forever fly free raised high in the air. ☒

I pledge allegiance to the flag
Of the United States of America
To the republic for which it stands
One nation under God, Indivisible
With liberty and justice for all.

Can you find the pledge in I Pledge My Allegiance?

America, How Sweet is Your Name

America, America, how sweet is your name
No other land equals your fame
Nations such as yours is all to few
There is no other that compares to you.

Home of eagles mighty and strong
Soaring though heaven in victor's song
Around the world with a heavy hand
Keeping peace with equitable demands.

Blessed with precious gems, silver and gold
More than King Solomon's temple could hold
To the world you open your food gates
Showing compassion from these United States.

From the Atlantic shores of Maine
To the Pacific islands of volcanic grains
Patrons gather for your anthem to sing
Listening to Liberty's bell in rhythm ring.

From southern beaches along Gulf of Mexico
To northern borders covered in snow
Many are called to share other's pain
And help their neighbor expecting no gain.

Thank you Lord, for those adorned in her uniform
And for a life sacrificed we truly mourn
I hope someday to shake their hand
In Heaven thank them for their courageous stand.

America's colors are red, white and blue
Honor and integrity waves beside truth
May her glorious symbol fly free and unfurled
Raised high upon her staff shining across the world. ©

Written by Gary Tucker
7-30-2011
©

Super Me

Who can leap tall buildings in a single bound?
Who can run faster than the speed of sound?
Who's stronger than a train and flies higher than a plane?
It's Super Me; let me explain.

Even though now I'm confined to this chair
With cloudy eyes and a heart needing repair
On the other side of death not far from here
I'll receive my new body and new clothes to wear.

I'll no longer need crutches to help me walk
I'll no longer need signs to help me talk
I'll no longer need glasses to help me see
An immortal body will be given to me.

Who can leap tall buildings in a single bound?
Who can run faster than the speed of sound?
Who's stronger than a train and flies higher than a plane?
It's Super Me; let me explain.

My new body will reflect God's glory
As laws of physics no longer control me
Without aid of transport I'll fly into space
And it's all because of God's wonderful grace.

I'll never grow old and I'll never die
No weapons to harm and no reasons why
All signs of warfare will disappear
We'll forever live in peace with no fear.

Who can leap tall buildings in a single bound?
Who can run faster than the speed of sound?
Who's stronger than a train and flies higher than a plane?
It's Super Me when I am changed. ©
Written by Gary Tucker 3-15-2011 ©

Little John

I heard a knock on the door
A man dressed in uniform
Said, "Your beloved had fallen
He was sorry to inform."

"He was so brave
Because of him I'm alive
Five men he saved
I'm one of the lucky five."

As I broke down in tears
He asked, "Is there family you can call?"
He tried to relieve my fears
My husband and I, that is all.

I knew this day might come
But, I was praying not today
Today's our anniversary
And there's a baby on the way.

As he spoke words of comfort
I saw tears form in his eyes
He began to tremble
And we both cried.

"Your husband and I were friends
He spoke with love of his Emily
Wish it were me instead of him
I have no family."

And that's how it began
Two weary souls
Became a new family
Not so long ago.

Together we raise Little John
He's proud to be his father's son.
In him his dad lives on
Reminding us of our fallen one. ©

Written by Gary Tucker
10-11-2010
©

Poems
of Love

True Love Never Parts

Burning embers start with sparks
Flaring in the depths of our hearts
Fanned by true loves' blowing
Constantly gleaming and glowing.

Beyond understanding but knowing
True love is always growing
Revealing tender feelings
True love is always showing.

Hearts are joined by one spark
That's how love always starts
Other emotions lose their devotion
But, true love never parts.

Crossing the barrier of time
True love developed refines
Tried and tested never reclines
True love matures sublime.

For true love many still seek
Peering into eyes of ones they meet
Searching their hearts for a spark
To see if true love can start.

Hearts are joined by one spark
That's how love always starts
Other emotions lose their devotion
But, true love never parts. ©

Written by Gary Tucker
5-21-2011 ©

My Little Boy Blue

They call him Blue, their five-year-old boy
He is their pride, their bundle of joy
With hair of gold and eyes so blue
Having fun in the park as they often do.

It was only a moment that dreadful day
Mom dropped her guard and Dad turned away
In a panic they ran to where he was playing
It was only a moment the swing was still swaying.

Mom started screaming as Dad yelled, too
Has anyone seen my little boy Blue?
With hair of gold and eyes so blue
Has anyone seen my little boy Blue?
With hair of gold and eyes so blue
Has anyone seen my little boy Blue?

The years took their toll and Mom fell ill
Finding Blue wasn't God's will
How long could she live with a heart so broke
After all the years she finally lost hope.

Dad made a promise before she died
Said he'd find Blue as he cried
His Blue was gone now his wife
How much more could he bear in this life?

Day after day the park Dad would visit
Passing the swing, he couldn't miss it
A dad and his boy were there to play
The dads shared a bench as it happened that day.

Surely they've met when they weren't as old
His eyes so blue and hair of gold
As dads were conversing young dad introduced
"Named after me this is my boy Blue."

Tears of joy filled Dad's eyes
He'd kept his promise then looked to the sky
Said, "Thank you Lord and please tell my wife
I finally found him, the joy of our lives."

My dad was shouting with a joyful sound
"He once was lost but now he's found
This is my boy, my little boy Blue
I finally found my little boy Blue."
"He once was lost but now he's found
I finally found my little boy Blue." ©

Written by Gary Tucker
9-2-2010
©

I'm so Sorry

Written by Gary Tucker ©
8-9-2011

Can't recall when we last loved
Seems we both have given up
Happiness shared was short lived
This selfish man, can you forgive?

I don't see smiles you use to wear
Your eyes are often filled with tears
We don't share dreams like before
You don't say you love me anymore.

I'm so sorry I caused you pain
I'm so sorry you feel ashamed
How could I have been so cruel?
Disregarding marriage rules.

Your silence cries out for help
Arms don't reach out to be held
Avoiding the need to be kissed
Past closeness is sorely missed.

Vainly thinking only of myself
Like a book put you on a shelf
You stood by me remaining true
To blind to see love for me in you.

Can you forgive this selfish man?
Can you love me as I am?
I promise to change my ways
And give you all my remaining days.

I'm so sorry I caused you pain
I'm so sorry you feel ashamed
How could I have been so cruel?
Disregarding marriage rules.

Can you forgive this selfish man?
Can you love me as I am?
I promise to change my ways
And give you all my remaining days. ©

My One And Only True Love

I never thought I could feel this way
You're on my mind all through the day
We fit together like a hand in glove
You are my one and only true love.

For you I wished upon a star
Now we're here in each other's arms
Until the end of time you'll always be
My one and only true love.

You're my night in shining armor
You're what my heart was pining for
A damsel waiting patiently
For my champion to reveal himself to me.

With true love to impart
You filled my empty heart
More and more bestowing
Beyond the point of overflowing.

The light in your eyes
Reflect love like a grand sunrise
Shining rays of color bright
A magnificent glorious sight.

The smiles you give to me
Are precious abundantly
Loving words you speak with ease
My ears hear them frequently.

Your touch is soft and gentle
Your kisses are plentiful
You treat me like a princess
With thoughtfulness and kindness.

You bring me pretty flowers
With lovely gifts you often shower
But, your love for this girl
I value more than priceless pearls.

I never thought I could feel this way
You're on my mind all through the day
We fit together like a hand in glove
You are my one and only true love.

For you I wished upon a star
Now we're here in each other's arms
Until the end of time you'll always be
My one and only true love. ©

Written by Gary Tucker
5-19-2011
©

America, America, Why Can't You See?

America, America, why can't you see
You once were a nation mighty and free
It wasn't long ago; remember when?
But, now your stars are glowing dim.

Your leaders have become corrupt and shallow
Their flattery words are empty and hollow
No one listens or respects them anymore
They've been caught stealing from your money stores.

In darkness sinners conspire to snuff out your life
By inciting your people with envy and strife
Your enemies dwell freely within your borders
Receiving commands with decisive orders.

You once stood for liberty and justice for all
Now your judges create their own laws
Detesting what the constitution declares
Arrogantly deeming it outdated and unfair.

By millions your littlest ones are dying
Disregarding precious life inside crying
Quietly it's all done out of sight
Because mothers are told it's their right.

Wake up Lady Liberty and open your eyes
Some among you spread deception and lies
Can't you see they plot your falling?
Remember your summons with holy calling.

God raised you up to shine across tidal seas
But, you scuttled your ship with no lifeguard to save thee
In much distress you're about to drown
Your once glorious symbol now flies upside down.

America, America, why can't you see?
A working lighthouse again you may be
Consider selecting servants in righteousness walking
Or sink electing criminals with the gift of double-talking. ©

Written by Gary Tucker
3-23-2011
©

"Ask not what America will do for you,
But rather what together we can do for the freedom of men."
USA President, John F. Kennedy

Some Don't Know

Some don't know the hell of battlegrounds
Where death and misery abounds all around
Some don't know the torture in my mind
When having to leave best friend behind.

Some don't know the heavy sorrow I bear
Never goers away, it's too painful to share
To find I harmed comrades in friendly fire
Do I end it now or escape from this mire?

Some don't know the angry words I hear
Departing the plane to screaming jeers
To be the object of ridicule robust
The placards say, "God hates your guts".

Some don't know and have no desire to learn
From right and wrong they can't discern
Some don't know evil must be fought
To love one's country they haven't been taught.

Some don't know for lack of knowledge
Protesting secured in their local college
While being bombarded with endless rounds
Our transport's been hit and we're going down.

Some don't know the meaning of honor
To stand upright they won't even ponder
Some don't know or care for their neighbor
Contempt and disgust in their hearts harbor.

Some don't know the conflicts raging inside
With each battle new monsters within hide
While I keep my demons under control
Some let theirs lose to wage a heavy toll.

Some don't know with missing leg or arm
How my scarred body causes stare and alarm
I returned home with a body sorely battered
Others returned with minds completely shattered.

Some don't know how to fight a war
They sit in an office demanding we give more
They make up silly rules and take away our guns
If it were up to them our wars would not be won.

Some don't know because to them it's unreal
When distant troubles are all but concealed
Waving white flag with surrender they find
While liberty and freedom is always on my mind.

Some don't know the horrific sounds of death
I will remember them till my final breath
Some don't know because they muted the sound
In the back of my head they forever resound.

Some don't know and they never will
Their cup of happiness will never be filled
I'm an American soldier in case you don't know
Humbled, as heartfelt gratitude overflows
from most. ©

Written by Gary Tucker
8-7-2011
©

Virtues

Before unlearned virtues come to late
Keep yourself pure when looking for a mate
Seek a virtuous man who desires to be holy
Flee from all others; seek godly ones only.

In regards to your attire
This virtue he should admire
Long, loose and lots
Don't show off what you've got.

In regards to your temple
This virtue is so simple
Knowledge and purity is wealth
Keep your hands and lips to your self.

In regards to your speech
Every pastor should preach
A virtue that shouldn't be buried
Don't speak as if you're married. ©

Written by Gary Tucker
10-31-2010
©

What Do You See?

What do you see
When you look into a mirror?
First clean the glass
So you can see clear.

Look past your face
Deep into your eyes
Ignore your surroundings
They only lie.

Down to your heart
So you can see the true you
Only there can you start
To see what you value.

Do you see envy?
Always wanting
Maybe there's pride
Always taunting.

For your neighbor
Does it care?
Will it raise
Him up in prayer?

Most importantly
Is it filled with love?
Does it have peace
With God above?

When you look at me
Do you see a potential friend?
Or are you unable to see past
The color of my skin?

Look past my face
Deep into my eyes
Ignore my surroundings
They only lie.

When you look into the mirror
What do you see?
Seeing a little clearer
Someone who's still better than me? ©

Written by Gary Tucker
10-23-2010
©

Oh Lord, Tell Me Why

About the author

In August 2010 I attempted to write down some poetic ideas to comfort my dear aunt. I found satisfaction knowing I can help others with a few chosen words. My desire is to lift up my neighbors near and far so they may have lasting benefits that begin in this life. I also enjoy writing about my home, The United States of America, what she has stood for in the past and what I believe her future holds.

It would be my pleasure to share with you my hopes and dreams Please let me know if I have succeeded at ohlordtellmewhy@aol.com.

You can read more of my poems in **I'm Feelin' Kinda Gassy,** which includes all of these poems plus fun poems, romantic poems with a twist and some for life's lessons.

May God bless you,
Gary L. Tucker